HOW TO HELP YOUR CHILD WITH MUSIC PRACTICE

A CRASH GUIDE FOR PARENTS

RUTH SEODI

PREFACE

I have been teaching the violin and piano to children and adults for over 20yrs. I've put close to 800 pupils through exams and had only two fails. Several pupils started with me around the age of 8yrs and continued right up to University where they continued their music studies. Very rewarding for me!

I've always tried to maintain regular contact with parents of my pupils, and have often and been asked for tips and help with regards to music practice at home between lessons.

Parents with little or no musical knowledge find it almost impossible to help their child at home, and consequently lesson time has often served to simply consolidate what was covered in the lesson the previous week, which clearly impedes progress and results in a loss of enthusiasm for the child over time.

Teachers are at the mercy of the parents in this regard, we can only do so much in terms of involving the parent and encouraging some playing at home between lessons.

I actually wrote the bulk of this book fifteen years ago but didn't pursue getting it published. So here I am in 2021 publishing this as an eBook which is so easily accessible to parents on a tablet or phone.

As the parent you play a key role in your child's musical progress, so I have written this book for you, to help you with your child's home practice.

I have learnt a lot over the years about how children learn and acquire new skills, and the methods I impart to you in this book are all workable and very successful.

Other books which I have written and are available on Amazon:

Time to Play a Musical Instrument, How to Take Up an Instrument Later in Life ISBN: 978-1-84528-342-1

Be Yourself, Ditch the Masks, 7 Steps to Unveiling Your True Self .ASIN:B01HY19T

CONTENTS

INTRODUCTION

Have you done your music practice?"

It's a line that's on every parent's lips if their child is learning to play a musical instrument, well every instrumental teacher hopes this is the case! If this phrase fills you with horror - because your child is unlikely to have done it, or you don't know how to help your child, then this guide is for you.

Your child may have come home from school with a letter in their book-bag about music lessons, or begged you to sign up for private instrumental lessons, and you might get all excited at the thought of watching your child evolve into a musical prodigy. However, when the reality of having to practice regularly at home between lessons sets in, there is often a decline in enthusiasm!

This Crash Guide for Parents will help you encourage your child to practice regularly, and also take the heat out of the "Have you done it yet?" rows.

Our daily lives are often so full, that finding the time and opportunity to practice isn't easy. It requires a commitment from both parent and child to ensure that a few minutes a day (or every other day) are allocated to music practice.

I've often recommended getting the child to draw their own weekly timetable of after school activities and build in a few minutes of music practice where possible. It's just a simple sheet of paper with the 7 days of the week and columns detailing the activities. Children enjoy creating it using different colours/little drawings etc. It's a gentle way of getting your child to take some responsibility for their practice time.

If your child is losing enthusiasm, this guide with help you (the parent), to rekindle it.

This book also provides you with a crash guide in the basics, such as notation, rhythm, time and expression, so you can give encouragement with some knowledge of what your child is supposed to be doing on a weekly basis. Many parents don't have a clue about music notes or other musical symbols and hence shy away from getting involved with their child's music.

I've written this book specifically to rectify this, and give you enough knowledge of the basics to assist your child with confidence. You might only be one step ahead of your child each week but that's enough to maintain a momentum with music practice.

There is a quick recap of the main points at the end of each chapter.

I have left a few blank pages at the end of the book for you to jot down any important points which may be particularly significant for you and your child. You can reference them as needed when assisting your child with music practice at home.

Why Do You Need This Guide?

I have been teaching music for over 20 years and I believe that regular practice is essential in determining a child's musical pleasure and success.

It's the quality not the quantity, of practice that really makes the difference. Poor practice leads to bad habits with the basics, such as inaccuracy, playing the wrong notes and not counting the beats correctly. Other bad habits are avoiding difficult sections and not reading instructions on the page properly. All of these will have to be corrected by the teacher during valuable weekly lesson time at your expense!

It would be far better for your child to achieve the week's practice targets set by the teacher, and see your child move forward.

The difference in morale and enthusiasm with a child who completes a piece, or learns new material each week rather than continually being asked to correct 'old ground', is very noticeable. It is the child's own perception of their progress which determines their enthusiasm for the instrument. No amount of praise from a parent or teacher can override the child's own recognition of self-improvement.

Some children are very self-critical, and can be hard on themselves unless what they are practising is absolutely correct. This type of child often has little patience, and can quickly become frustrated. They are usually very bright children who aspire to high standards of achievement.

In such cases, I have found the best approach is short bursts of focused practice on the piece in hand, (it may be as little as two or four bars - a quarter or half a line of music), followed by a 'fun-play' through of a piece already mastered of their own choice. You may manage two or three cycles of alternating in this way in a 20 or 30minute practice.

Low self - esteem is another characteristic which requires careful handling during practice. In such a case, plenty of praise works well. It's better to ignore some of the inaccuracies in rhythm and simply aim for correct notes initially, or aim for an accurate rhythm and ignore some note errors. Again two or four bars or a quarter or half a line of music is enough to work on.

Providing your child appears pleased with his/her achievement, you can then go back over the same section and add or correct any other instructions. The key is to observe your child's mood and act accordingly...either continue with the next two or four bars or take a break and move onto something they have previously mastered of their own choice.

We are ultimately aiming for your child to practice independently without too much 'hand holding'. To reach this point we have to nurture confidence and good practice habits

CHAPTER ONE

Practice - Pleasure or chore?

You don't need me to tell you that self -discipline in a child doesn't always come naturally. Yet it is such an advantage when it comes to focusing on school work and homework! Your child may prefer the excitement of their latest computer game, iPad, mobile phone etc. All these distractions are increasingly difficult to compete with, particularly when it comes to encouraging your child to do their music practice on a regular basis.

A child's attention span will vary depending on their age and development. If left alone to practice in the early stages, your child will be unlikely to have any structure to the session. They may prefer to cut the practice short and look for something else to grab their attention - something which will give them more of a 'quick fix'.

So what can you do?

Sitting with your child during practice will give some adult interaction, with structure, encouragement and quality one to one time. You can also check how accurately they are playing and help with any difficulties. Everything you need to know about notes and rhythm etc. is covered later on in this book. I know this takes time, maybe you could get on with some other jobs providing you are within earshot.

Once you have established a good pattern of practice, and you feel your child is showing signs of being able apply the techniques I have outlined in this guide, you can begin to encourage your child to do alternate practice sessions on their own. Then you can acknowledge their achievements as they occur. If you find that this new routine isn't working so well, then go back to what you were doing before and sit in on every practice for a little longer. If, however, your child does well with the new regime gradually reduce your time even further.

If you follow the practice tips in this guide, your child should see for himself/herself that they are moving forward.

Chapter Two, *What every parent needs to know* should see you through the first three to six months of your child's lessons. Learning to play an instrument gives children confidence and provides a healthy educational challenge. It will also help children to apply the same self-disciplined approach to other areas of their lives.

Practice can easily become a drudgery or a chore. For some children who have little or no support at home during practice, their only motivation is to 'please the teacher' at the next lesson. This may be enough to keep the child going in the short term, but a child needs more to encourage them each week in the longer term. That's where an important sense of achievement at the end of each practice comes in. Encouraging your child to set small achievable targets for each practice session is the key. Ideally your child should feel good at the end of each practice session, feeling a sense of achievement from the progress they've made.

Young children (aged 5-7) really benefit from an adult by their side for at least part of their music practice. They love to show a parent what they can play and what they covered in their lesson. Older children might take to getting on with it by themselves, but knowing that you're on hand to help out would be a great comfort.

Many music teachers jot down what they want your child to try each week. Some give more detailed notes than others! Some don't write anything at all! In such a case I advise you get in touch with the music teacher and request that they write clear and simple practice requests in a note book. You and your child can refer to this regularly and tick off the items that have been done successfully and perhaps make a note of any difficulties so that the teacher can address them in the next lesson.

At the start of covid I switched to teaching on zoom, and my pupils had to jot down the practice requests for the week themselves. I often dictated to them but it certainly made a difference because they had written the notes themselves. Now that I'm doing some face to face teaching again I've decided to continue this system of the pupil writing their own notes in the practice book themselves.

Most children will rise to a challenge if they feel they can achieve it reasonably easily. Ideally, each practice session will give them enough of the 'feel good' factor to motivate them onto the next.

However, if your child starts a piece on the wrong note and they can hear that it sounds wrong, it's enough to put them off trying it again for the rest of the week. Working out how to correct that wrong starting note is very simple and would only take you a couple of minutes to work it out with your child. I cover how to do this later on in the book. If you can be on hand to help out like this, then you'll be able to get your child back on track and moving forward without a whole week wasted because your child didn't have the motivation or help to sort out the problem.

It's always best to have the first home practice as soon after the lesson as possible. It's all fresher in the mind and memory, and gives a good kick start to the 7 days until the next lesson.

There's nothing worse than leaving it until the day before the lesson...the teacher will see through this, trust me!

On Their Own?

Practicing can be a lonely experience. The child is often banished from the hub of the family, especially if it involves playing the piano, which might well be in a separate room. They might have to struggle with difficulties in the music and attempt new skills which may take some mastering. Unless the child is exceptionally dedicated, these conditions are not conducive to enormous amounts of pleasure or satisfaction.

If your child plays on a keyboard, then headphones allow him/her to play without leaving the main family room. However other instruments don't have this benefit and require your child to move into a room alone.

You, the parent, have committed to paying for lessons, music and instrument, not to mention repairs! But if you don't get the practice sessions right, then your investment could be going down the drain! So spend time getting involved with your child's practice. Transform what can be a lonely solitary experience, into something positive where you and your child can share the pleasure in learning music together even if it's just for the first 5 minutes of the practice session.

I've often suggested to parents that they video a little performance of their child playing a piece, you can send it to relatives and give your child's accomplishment a real sense of importance. Most children like being photographed or videoed, they are the centre of attention, so remember this as being something you can use to give your child a target to complete a piece to send to Grandma, Auntie etc. The following chapters address ways in which you can help your child see that practice can be fun, and that being able to play a musical instrument is a valuable, enjoyable and lifelong skill.

Quick Recap

- The quality of practice is more important than the quantity.
- Try not to pick up bad practice habits – don't avoid the difficult bits, and really look at what's on the page!
- If practice is tough going, then break it up with fun tunes of your child's choice.
- Observe your child's mood and give lots of praise and encouragement.
- Sit with your child during practice and enjoy this learning time together.
- Take photos/videos when your child has completed a piece and send it to loved ones.
- .

CHAPTER TWO

What Every Parent Needs to Know

Keeping The Beat.

You can probably tap your foot to a beat when listening to music. but can you keep a regular and even beat like the ticking of a clock? This is what your child needs to achieve with music pieces. Don't allow your child to play the easy bits fast and the difficult bits slow, which is often the temptation, - even if it means playing the piece at 'snail's pace', avoid mixing fast and slow.

Some notes are long; some are short. Each one has to be counted, according to its value.

Some pieces have a fast beat, some have a slow beat but for elementary pieces it's more about what your child's comfort speed is! Easy pieces will probably be played at top speed but more challenging pieces are likely to be played more slowly (except the easy bits which will take on a faster speed!) Keeping the beat is all about maintaining a steady speed. It requires a little self- discipline to resist speeding up for the easy bits.

Musicians often use a tool called a metronome to set the speed of a piece. Even professional musicians use them when learning a new piece. It ticks (like a clock) at the required speed to help you keep the beat steady. There are plenty of free metronome Apps available, I strongly recommend you download one and use it with your child. It's fun and easy to work with, and will be a novelty to add into the practice regime. Pieces will often have what we call a 'metronome marking' in the top left corner of a piece. Here's an example:

$\downarrow = 120$ This example shows that the metronome should tick 120 times per minute (so twice per second). We set the metronome to the appropriate speed depending on how fast or slow the piece needs to be.

Ideally your child will reach the point when they can feel the beat, either in the body, or tapping the foot or simply counting at a regular speed, but this skill comes with practice and a metronome is a good way of introducing how to do this.

The following section covers the note values, what they look like and how to count them.

How to Count the Beats

We decide how long to hold notes on by counting the beats. Some notes are short, so just one beat or less, and some notes are long. These can be held on while counting 3 or 4 beats.

These are the basic note values which your child will cover during the early stages of learning.

note value	notes
4 beats =	○
2 beats =	♩
1 beat =	♩
$\frac{1}{2}$ beat =	♪

The names, Minim (2 beats) and dotted Minim (3 beats) are easy to remember together. The Semibreve however isn't so easy to remember unless you understand a bit of history about it, which I'll explain.

Back in Medieval times they used a note called a Breve, which lasted for 8 beats. We no longer use this note value, but the Semibreve, (semi - meaning half) is the 4 beat note - half of a Breve, which is often used in music today. Children tend to remember the word 'quaver' easily, as it's the same name as a crispy snack!

Notes are divided into equal groups of beats by lines. These are called **bar-lines**. The spaces between the bar lines are called **bars**. We count the beats as we go along, always starting at beat number 1 again, when we cross a bar-line into a new bar.

All of the pieces and exercises your child will come across in the elementary stages of learning always share the same number of beats in every bar. So once you see how many beats there are in every bar - which is explained the next section called 'Time Signature', you simply have to keep counting up to that number,

6

being sure to start at 1 again at the start of every new bar.

Here are 3 bar lines and 4 bars with a double line at the end. The double line tells us it's the end of the piece. The numbers at the start are called a *Time Signature* and are covered in the next section.

Time Signature - what does it mean?

You will always find two numbers at the beginning of a piece of music. This is called the *time signature*. In the following example, the top number designates how many beats there are in each bar. This number is usually a 2, 3 or 4. The bottom number need not be explained at this stage as it's a bit more complex, but in elementary music the bottom number will be a 4. It's the top number which is important to grasp here.

Any combination of note values can be used in a bar as long as each bar adds up to the upper number in the time signature.

Here's an example:

The numbers below the notes show where the beats fall in each bar. Your child may be given a piece which has the letter C instead of the usual numbered time signature. This C represents 4 beats to be counted in every bar, and is often referred to as *'common time'* and looks like this:

It dates back to the period when time signatures were represented by full circles, and half circles, (back in Medieval times). The full circle indicates 8 beats in every bar - so it would include the long Breve note which has 8 counts, and the half circle indicates 4 beats in every bar. (We no long have the option of 8 beats in a bar). In this case the C represents the half circle. The half circle has evolved over the centuries into the letter C and was named *'common time'*.

Does a Quaver make you quiver?

The Quaver is worth half a beat, so two quavers fit into one whole beat. They usually come in pairs in elementary pieces and are joined by a line across the top. We call this line a *'beam'*.

I often find that using a word with two syllables often helps children get the quaver rhythm right. Words like, coff-ee or run-ning. Here's an example of what I mean.

Walk   Walk   Run - ning Run - ning

For the one beat notes you could use 'Tea Tea' and for the quavers 'coff-ee coff-ee'.

A semibreve is the hardest note name to remember, as I discovered with a six- year- old pupil many years ago, when I was testing her memory on these words. "And what is the 4 beat note called?" I asked. She replied: "A semi breath"!

She clearly thought I couldn't pronounce my 'th's'!

The term semibreve is best understood and remembered by becoming familiar with the breve, which is held for 8 beats. Such long notes have now fallen into disuse, but *semibreve* clearly means half a *breve* hence 4 beats long.

Dots After Notes

You may have already come to realise that music notation is very precise - it has to be written and read with accuracy. A dot in the wrong place can alter a note or bar to the extent that it doesn't make any sense at all!

A dot after a note makes it half as long again. This is worth knowing and remembering. The dot requires you to add on half of the value of the note it is next to.

So for example, a dotted quaver becomes three quarters of a beat, (half a beat plus a quarter of a beat). A crotchet worth one beat, becomes one and a half beats with a dot beside it. A minim, which is worth two beats, becomes a three beat note if it has a dot next to it. What would the value of a semibreve be if it had a dot placed next to it?

All these dotted notes change their names into dotted quaver, dotted crotchet, dotted minim, and a dotted semibreve. With the dotted crotchet you may be wondering what happens with the remaining half beat - well it's usually followed either by a quaver note or a quaver rest, which is worth half a beat, rounding it up to two beats altogether.

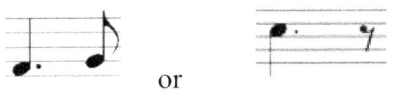

or

Dots can also be placed next to rests. They work in exactly the same way as with notes - adding on half of the value of the note. These dots are always placed to the right of the note or rest. So if your child is a budding composer make sure the dot is placed correctly on the right side of the note/rest, not the left!

The Sound of Silence.

Sometimes there are places where no note is played, and silence is required. Again, these silences are measured in beats. These silences are called *rests*. Here, I've shown the various rests which match the different beat lengths of the notes covered above. You will notice that I have used the five parallel lines in this example. This is called a *stave or staff.*

Rest	Length
	4 beats
	2 beats
	1 beat
	1/2 beat
	1/4 beat

Please note that the semibreve rest is also used as a whole bar rest which means it looks the same whether there are 2, 3 or 4 beats in every bar.

Here's an example of notes and rests combined. See how each bar adds up to 4 crotchet beats.

There are of course many more note values used in music. However, those covered so far, will see you through the early stages of your child's music practice.

Quick Recap

- Keep a regular even beat like the ticking of a clock
- Use the time signature to find out how many beats in there are in a bar. Count the beats as you go along.
- Beats are divided up into **bars** by **bar-lines**.
- A 'C next to the clef means you have four beats in a bar (known as common time).
- Learn and use the correct terminology.
- Rests are as important as notes when counting the beats.

CHAPTER THREE

Knowing The Notes.

All notes must be drawn on a line or in a space on the music stave/staff. Some instruments use different clefs. In the next section of this chapter you'll find which clef applies to your child's instrument. Here are the clefs we use for different instruments. I've stuck to the most popular instruments that children learn...however, there are others that I haven't covered here. We use different clefs to accommodate the pitch of the instrument.

The Treble Clef is used for high sounding instruments. The Alto Clef is used for middle range instruments, and the Bass Clef for the low sounding instruments.

Treble clef   Bass clef   Alto clef

Treble Clef: Flute, Violin, Trumpet, Recorder, Clarinet, Guitar, Ukulele, Piano
Bass Clef: Cello, Trombone, Piano
Alto Clef: Viola

Each note has a letter name between A and G. If the notes climb up the stave as in the example above, then you ascend the alphabet letters. If the notes descend on the stave, then you go down/backwards in the alphabet. I haven't used a clef in the image above as I simply wanted to demonstrate how the notes use every line and space on a stave.

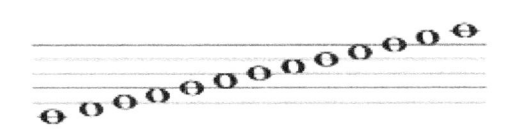

You'll notice that the first and last note have a line through the middle. This line is used for notes which are too high or too low to fit within the stave (which only ever has 5 lines and 4 spaces). These extra lines are called *ledger lines*. You can have more than one ledger line depending on how much higher or lower the note is outside of the 5 stave lines.

Having reached G, you count up again starting from A. This time though, the notes will have a higher sounding pitch since they are higher up on the stave.

For example, most pianos have seven 'blocks' of A to G. If you count the white notes from the left side, you will find seven blocks of A to G take you to the very top of the piano (to the right), measuring 49 white notes in all. (This is a general guide, and some pianos have reduced or extended length).

One of the clefs shown earlier in this section, will appear at the very beginning of the *stave*. I included three different clefs which cover most of the popular instruments that children learn. Of course those of you who have a pianist in the family will need to be familiar with both the treble and bass clefs. Commonly taught instruments like the violin, flute, guitar, recorder will just read from one stave which has a treble clef at the start.

Children who play the cello will also have one stave but will see the bass clef at the start of each line. Pianists will have two staves with a treble clef at the start of the top line for the right hand which plays the higher sounding notes, and a bass clef at the start of the bottom line for the left hand which plays the lower sounding notes.

How to recognise note names for clefs.

In the case of piano or keyboard both the treble clef and bass clef are used.

The purpose of a *clef* is to keep the notes within the lines and spaces of the stave where possible, for easy reading. Instruments vary in pitch. For example, a double bass plays low notes and a flute or a violin play high notes. So a clef fixes a note on the stave to suit the pitch of an instrument or group of instruments.

The term 'Middle C' is often used as a kind of anchor, to show which side of Middle C a particular note falls. On a full size piano there are seven C notes in total and the term 'Middle C' denotes the C that is midway between the top and bottom of the keyboard.

 The treble clef is used for higher sounding instruments such as the *violin, flute, recorder, guitar, recorder, trumpet Ukulele and Piano*. It fixes the note G, (above middle C), on the second line up from the bottom, on the stave. Notice how the clef curls around that second line up from the bottom, which marks where the G note would sit.

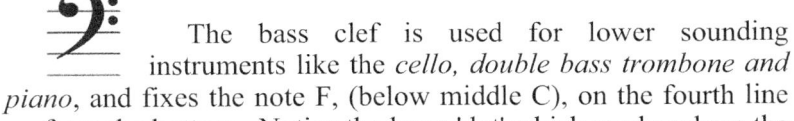 The bass clef is used for lower sounding instruments like the *cello, double bass trombone and piano*, and fixes the note F, (below middle C), on the fourth line up from the bottom. Notice the large 'dot' which marks where the F note goes.

 The alto clef used for the *viola*, places middle C on the middle stave line (right between the two curves

of the clef).

These are the note names for each different clef. Try getting to know the notes of the clef that appear on your child's music.

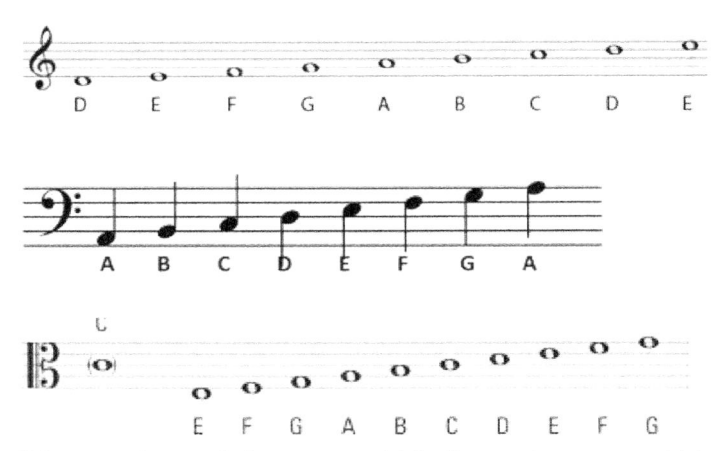

I have only used the notes which fit on the stave within the printed lines and spaces. Notes can however be lower or higher than the stave accommodates. For example:

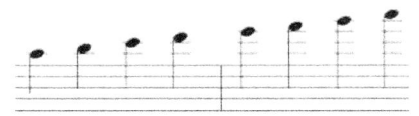

In order to measure exactly which space or line the note fits on, small 'extra' lines are used. These extra lines are spaced the same distance apart as those on the stave. These extra lines are called **ledger lines.**

Some children find it helpful to make up a word or a memorable sentence to help with the note learning. Here's an example for each different clef. There are of course many variations on these sentences, and your child may enjoy making up one of their own for the clef(s) they are reading from.

G B D F   For the alto clef you can use 'Great Big Dragonflies Fly'.

Lines and spaces are used for music notes. To work out the ones in between, simply go up one or down one letter to work it out.

In the examples above, you will notice some tails pointing downwards and some point upwards. The basic rule is that notes below the middle line on the stave, should have tails pointing upwards. The notes above the middle line on the stave, have their tails pointing downwards. Those notes which are on the middle line may go either way. However, they should follow those tails which appear immediately before or after.

I have come across children who think the top or bottom of the tail indicates which note to play. I have often wondered what significance they think the circle has in that case! Be watchful and make sure your child is reading from the circles not the tails.

Quick Recap

- Notes are from A to G. Go up or down the alphabet depending on the direction of the notes.
- Recognise which *clef* your child is using.
- Use simple sentences to help learn the note names.
- Read from the circles not the tails
-

CHAPTER FOUR

Sharps, Flats and Naturals -what are they?

The word *accidental* is a generic term for the *flat, sharp* and *natural* sign. When printed on the stave they look like this:

Flat sign   Sharp sign   Natural sign

These symbols are placed on lines or in spaces in the same way that notes are. This enables us to identify which note the flat, sharp or natural relates to. Here's an example.

The flat requires you to *lower* the note to exactly half way between the note you are on and the next note below. On the piano this usually involves playing a black note. On a stringed instrument you would slide the finger back slightly.

The sharp sign requires you to raise the note *higher*, exactly half way towards the next note up.

The natural sign cancels out a previous sharp or flat for a particular note, returning it to its normal pitch.

An accidental is valid for the whole bar in which it appears. Once you cross the bar-line into a new bar, the accidental is no longer valid. If there is more than one of the same note which has the accidental next to it, then it must also be made sharp or flat.

There are actually more than these three accidentals covered here. However, you are not likely to come across any others at the early stages of learning.

The sharp or flat can also appear at the very beginning of a piece, next to the clef sign. In this case the accidental(s) are valid for the whole piece. You will not have a kind reminder of the flat, sharp or natural just before the note it applies to - you just have to remember!

As the natural sign has a different purpose to the sharp and flat it does not appear next to the clef as part of a key signature at the very start of a piece.

Key Signatures. What Key is the Music in?

Sharps or flats placed immediately next to the clef are called a key signature.

You may have come across classical pieces titled 'Concerto in G Major', or 'Symphony in D Minor'. These are both names of keys. Each key has its own unique key signature, and we use the key signature at the start of a piece to identify which sharps or flats are required to be played in that piece. Just one sharp means that all the Fs in the piece have to be played as F sharps. Two sharps, means all the Fs and Cs have to be played as sharps, (on the piano this means playing black notes). One flat means all the B's have to played as B flats. Two flats, means that all the B's and E's have to be played as flats, (again on the piano this involves black notes).

A key signature will never mix sharps and flats. It will always be one or the other. In the early stages of learning, you will not usually find more than one or two sharps or flats in a key signature.

If your child is playing a piece with a key signature you may find that you have to remind them to play the appropriate sharps or flats. It's easy to forget them in the early stages.

It's very common in easy elementary pieces to have no sharps or flats next the clef. In this case the piece is in the key of C major. In the case of the piano it means there are no black notes to play. In the key of C major all the notes are what we call *naturals*. Please note that I've kept this section very simple, and for anyone reading this who has a good knowledge of music they will note that I have omitted anything to do with what we call minor keys. I didn't want to complicate it any further by introducing the minor keys.

Heavy on the Scales

Scales are the backbone of learning any instrument. They key that a composer chooses to use for a particular piece is based on the notes of a specific scale. The composer may add accidentals to notes (extra sharps or flats), and veer off the main scale momentarily in order to create the melody he/she wants, but on the whole, the notes of the piece will be based on the notes of the scale designated by the chosen key. It's not uncommon to find a change of key within a piece, in which case there would be a clear instruction to the player, by showing a new key signature - the notes which follow must be played according to the new key signature.

There are various types of scale, all of which have a slightly different sounds. Notes ascend to the top and descend to the bottom - their unique sound depends on the distances in pitch between each note.

Eastern music for example, has a very recognisable sound and is based on scales that have a totally different template to scales in Western music.

There are three common scales that your child is likely to come across, especially when preparing for face to face music examinations. These are the major scale, and the minor scale. The minor scale can be in the melodic or harmonic version.

Here's an example of a simple major scale:

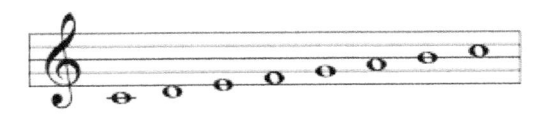

It starts on C and ends on C and has no sharps or flats. Nice and easy to play on a keyboard or piano as it's all white notes!

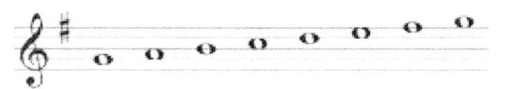

This scale starts on G and ends on G and has F sharps. It is called the G major scale.

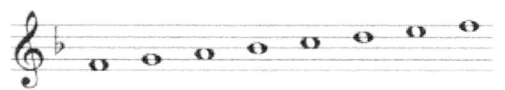

This scale starts on F and ends on F and has B flats. It's called the F major scale.

Your child's knowledge and use of scales will depend very much on the teacher, as some will be heavier on scales than others. However, scales are very important, especially when it comes to learning pieces and preparing for music examinations. They are used to learn finger positions on an instrument and for string and wind players, they help improve accurate tuning and your child's sense of pitch.

Scales are also a useful tool for working on finger dexterity - the ability to move fingers quickly and accurately. They will also help your child get used to finger placement on the different keys or strings. All of these benefits combine to build your child's playing skills and enable your child to master pieces at a faster rate with more knowledge, understanding and confidence.

No doubt by now you will have deduced that I'm a strong advocate of learning scales! They are an invaluable tool when it comes to learning a musical instrument.

Quick Recap

- Accidentals are sharps flats and naturals.
- You can recognise which note an accidental applies to, by looking at the line or space it is printed on.
- Accidentals are valid for a whole bar. Once you cross a bar-line they are no longer applicable.
- A key signature tells you which sharps or flats apply for the whole piece. You have to remember these!
- Every piece is in a particular key. It's the key signature that decides what key your piece is in.

CHAPTER FIVE

Express Yourself!

This is the 'icing on the cake', where your child can make the music his/her own and add some musical interpretation. When your child has learnt the notes and rhythm of a piece, and can play it confidently, he/she can begin to include the expression markings, such as changes of speed, volume and phrasing.

Most instructions of expression originate from Italy. Many of the most important early composers in the Renaissance Period flocked to Italy, it was a haven for musicians and composers. It was during this period that numerous expression markings were used extensively and became popular for the first time. We still use the Italian terms of expression today, so you and your child will need to learn a little Italian!

These Italian terms are often abbreviated down to the first letter. Those which relate to volume changes are grouped under the generic label, dynamics. Below are the ones you are most likely to find in your child's practice pieces.

There are of course many more, but those listed here will meet your needs in the early stages of learning.

Children get quickly used to their own comfort speed and level of loudness. They tend to play everything at the same levels, so when it comes to introducing different speed changes and levels of loud and soft playing it can be challenging. Every instrument requires different techniques to build in loud and soft playing so it will be up to the teacher as to when your child starts to add the different expression markings noted in this table.

Even the very first music examinations such as the ABRSM's Prep Test and Initial Grade (both of which I cover in detail in chapter 8) require these basic musical expression instructions to be demonstrated.

Abbreviation	Italian	English
P	Piano	Quiet
PP	Pianissimo	Very quiet
M	Mezzo	Half
F	Forte	Loud
FF	Fortissimo	Very loud
MP	Mezzo piano	Half quiet
MF	Mezzo forte	Half loud
Rit	Ritenuto	Get slower
Rall	Rallentando	Get slower
Accel	Accelerando	Get quicker
Dim	Diminuendo	Gradually get quieter
Cresc	Crescendo	Gradually get louder
DC	Da Capo	Go back to the beginning
A Tempo	A Tempo	Back to the original speed
Fine	Fine	The end

Other symbols used

Common Symbols

Pause	⌢	Hold the note for longer than its value. At player's discretion
Repeat	:|	Back to the beginning or previous repeat sign
1st time bar	1.	1st time through: play this bar
2nd time bar	2.	2nd time through: play this bar
Gradually get louder		
Gradually get softer		

Musical Punctuation, Phrasing

Some of your child's music may have long curved lines above groups of notes. Here's an example:

These lines are called ***phrase marks***. They serve the same purpose as commas and full stops in text. They group the notes into a 'musical sentence' or ***phrase***, transforming a piece of music from a string of notes to a beautiful melody with shape.

Phrase endings should be 'rounded off' gracefully, just as you might end a verse of a poem or a song. Phrases are generally two or four bars long. Some children find phrasing very easy and are able to include it naturally in their playing. Others find it more difficult and have to know the piece really well before they can follow their sense of phrasing.

Many pieces don't have any phrase marks printed at all, so it's up to your child to work out where phrases end and begin. To be honest in the early stages of learning, phrasing isn't really a strong focus, but when your child moves from the elementary to intermediate stage of learning then an understanding of phrasing will become important.

The Slur

The ***slur*** looks similar in appearance to the phrase mark. It is a curved line above or below two notes or more. However, it serves a totally different purpose to the phrase mark. For string players, it means your child has to use one bow stroke for the slurred notes. for wind players, pianists and singers the notes have to be joined smoothly without a break in the sound. Here's an example of slurs:

Quick Recap

- Help your child to know the abbreviated expression markings.
- Encourage your child to think about the phrasing of piece (once the notes/rhythm are in place)
- Note the difference between slurs and phrase mark

CHAPTER SIX

Practice Tips

"Have you done your practice yet?

If you dread practice time, this chapter will help you encourage your child.

Start off by sitting with your child making yourselves comfortable. If your child really doesn't like you observing so closely, then just 'hover' nearby and listen. If your child is using a music stand, make sure it's the right height, at eye level, and positioned so you can both see it. Always have a pencil handy to write any little pointers on the music that might help as they go along. If you are short of time, just make the most of it and try not to let that affect or spoil the practice session.

Remember, a little practice is always better than none!

For little ones (aged 5-7), I suggest four or five 10-15min practices. For older children, (7-9 yrs), aim for 15-20 min practices four or five times a week. Increase the practice time as your child gets older and progresses further.

You can set a timer on your phone or tablet if necessary, although there's nothing worse than your child just playing for playing sake until the timer goes off!

I've found that asking your child to make a little practice timetable works well (as I mentioned in an earlier chapter). They can get creative with colours and drawings - just ask your child to write the days of the week across the top, then add in any after school activities and look for some small gaps of time when music practice can be done.

Tick off each practice completed and maybe set up some kind of reward chart.

If the piece your child is practising is new, then I suggest you point out any errors as you go along. However, if the piece isn't new, then allow your child to play it to the end even if you notice errors. This allows you to pick up any underlying misunderstanding that might be common to the errors. For example, your child may not have grasped how to count the beats properly, or your child might regularly mistake a G for a B,(or something similar).

In these situations, you can refer back to the earlier chapters of this guide and correct their understanding.

Once your child feels all the errors have been corrected, do allow a performance from start to finish. Hopefully it will all be correct. However, if it isn't, still let your child play to the end. It can be very disheartening to be stopped many times when you feel you can play it, and have put time and effort into learning and practicing it.

Repeat, Repeat, Repeat

One key factor in practice, is repetition of difficult sections of a piece. If your child makes the same mistake over and over again, it will do more harm than good. The fingers will soon get used to making the error and very quickly build that wrong note or rhythm into the piece. Your child will soon be totally unaware of the mistake.

These errors then change into habits, which can take time to undo. Catching mistakes early can avoid this. Playing a section over and over which is error free however, allows the fingers to get used to it. Very soon the fingers begin to play without needing so much thought and concentration. It is at this point that your child can relax with the piece and enjoy making it 'his/her own' by adding expression like louds and softs, phrasing and any speed changes that are noted in the piece. Catch mistakes early and avoid them becoming a habit!

Establishing good practice techniques at an early age is vital to your child's progress. It will boost confidence, and speed up the journey through the graded exams. Your children should look forward to lessons, and showing their teachers what they have achieved during the week.

If your child starts saying they don't want lessons any more, ask yourself if there's a problem with the practice routine first, rather than the teacher.

Children know when they haven't practiced correctly, or enough, and feelings of guilt can creep in. This alone, is enough to put a child off lessons.

Games

Try testing each other, using a whiteboard, blackboard or paper and pencil. Get your child to roleplay being the teacher and you roleplay the pupil. Pretend to get things wrong and encourage your child to spot your mistakes. Allow them to correct you. Children love correcting adults!

You can test each other on note values by mixing up the beat values and jotting them down on a piece of paper in numbers, (2 4 1 3 for example), and get your child to draw the right note above the right number.

If your child doesn't get it right, explain where they went wrong and try again. You can do this four or five times before moving on. Aim for a couple of consecutive correct answers.

If your child showed a weakness in this little exercise, then do build it into your music time again and again until it's really well known.

Note names can also be tested, by drawing a stave, (five parallel lines) and writing some note names underneath. Your child has to draw the correct note on the stave above the note name. You can switch roles after two or three goes each, and before you know it you've done a good twenty- minute session, consolidating your child's understanding and having fun at the same time!

You can improve rhythm by opening the music book at any page and asking your child to clap the rhythm of two or three bars. You can refer to Chapter Two which covers the note values and suggests using words such as 'Walk Walk' for the one beat notes (crotchets), and 'Run-ning Run-ning' for the half beat notes (quavers).

Other words work well too, like 'Pear Pear', 'App-le App-le', or 'Cat Cat', 'Dogg-ie Dogg-ie'. There are endless combinations of words to use.

It can be fun making up names of your own, using a pet's name for example.

If you want to print off some blank music manuscript paper to help with these games, then you can print it for free if you go to https://www.blanksheetmusic.net/

Fifteen minutes a day is far better than thirty minutes every other day, and certainly better than a last-minute practice just before the lesson!

If your child doesn't want to practice regularly, suggest a play through of some pieces already mastered in the past. It's always better to play something than nothing, and going over favourite tunes, (or ones that come easily to them), will help build confidence and motivation, and serve as a reminder that playing a musical instrument brings pleasure and fun!

Theory and Practice.

Encourage your child to draw notes on music manuscript paper and play them to you. This is a great way of consolidating what your child knows, and adding some variety, as are the games mentioned earlier in this chapter. It will also raise self-esteem and make them feel like a 'real' composer.

Encourage your child to include as much detail as possible. such as time signature, bar-lines, varying rhythms, musical expression and even phrase marks. Let their imagination work creatively. Suggest they create a title for the piece...you may have the makings of a little Mozart!

Slowly Does It!

Children often expect to be able to play something right, at the correct speed on the first attempt. This is where children often set themselves up for failure and disappointment. Their young, less mature minds find it hard to be patient, and the thought of doing it slowly, goes against the grain.

Instead, give them a target of playing it through three times slowly. When they've done this without making a mistake they can notch up the speed slightly. Your child will then gradually work up to the correct speed.

If they can't play it right slowly then they certainly can't play it right fast!

Try breaking the music down by focusing firstly on the rhythm, then the notes. The rhythm should be clapped or tapped out or played on one single note.

How do you do this? Look at how many beats there are in a bar at the beginning of the piece in the time signature. It will have a 2, 3 or 4 as the top number in the time signature.

Remember, it's the upper number in the time signature which indicates how many beats in every bar. Count yourself an 'empty' bar of beats to set the speed before your child begins to tap out the rhythm. If there are two beats in a bar for example, say out loud "one, two," and tap your hand at the same time before your child begins to play. The piece should be played to the speed of your 'tap'.

Set a fairly slow speed to start off with - one count per second is a rough guide.

Here's an example of how you and your child might tap out a simple rhythm. In each bar, the notes add up to three beats. I've also added a reminder of the note values to guide you.

The bar-lines separate the notes into groups with equal amounts of beats. Children often make the mistake of pausing or hesitating at a bar-line. Try to stop them doing this! The speed of the beat should keep going throughout, without hesitations at bar-lines.

Rhythmic Words

If your child is finding it difficult to tap or clap the rhythm to the beat, use the rhythmic words as a quick fix-it. See the earlier section in the Chapter headed 'Games'. I gave lots of examples.

If your child comes up with different words, then it's far more likely that your child will use them in a regular practice session. I've used this method for many years with pupils and found it to be very successful. Once your child gets the rhythm right a few times using the words then you have success and the words no longer need to be used. It's a really useful tool to use whenever the rhythm seems challenging.

Remember also that clapping the rhythm and saying the rhythmic words at the same time also works well.

In the earlier section called Games, I referred to words for 1 beat notes and 2 beat notes. If your child has a group of 4 quavers, you could either repeat the 'run-ning' or 'app-le', or 'dogg-ie' words twice, or choose a word with four syllables, like 'pom-e-gran-ate', or 'capp-u-ccin-o' for example.

Often, when children see quavers joined, up they play them leaving a small gap, or hesitation after each pair or group. I can see why they do it. It's a visual thing, but it's worth pointing out that they need to stick to the beat and speed of the piece while counting

Keep counting, and stick to the beat without hesitations!

Teach The Fingers Where to Go

If you can touch type - type without looking at your fingers - you'll understand how it feels when your fingers know where to go. It's like this with an instrument. Fingers do actually 'learn' where to go, if they are shown enough times. However, if the fingers are not doing exactly what's on the page then they learn inaccurately. So it's very important to iron out any mistakes early on.

Keep the pace slow, until the fingers thoroughly know the notes. The more errors a child makes when learning something new, the longer it will take to get it consistently right.

To get your child going, help by working out the name of the first note, and find it on the instrument. Then decide if the next note is higher or lower using the alphabet, and how many places higher or lower. Remember that we only use the first seven alphabet letters to name notes, and after the note G, we return to A. Begin to get familiar with these notes, what they look like on the stave and where they are on the instrument.

Here's an example.

E to F = go up 1 note. F to F = same note. F to A = go up 2 notes. A to G = go down 1 note. G to E = go down 2

It's very important to know the note names. One way is to use a game mentioned earlier in this chapter where your child draws notes that are already known, on manuscript paper (you can simply draw the 5 stave lines on a piece of paper if you don't have manuscript), or on a whiteboard. You then have to label them correctly! Your child can then tick or cross your answers.

Getting a few deliberately wrong can give your child the pleasure of correcting you! Then swap over.

Timing each other is another good way to learn note names. How quickly can you label them all correctly? After all, when practising a piece your child will need to find and play the correct notes quickly.

Invest some, time early on in learning the note names and finding them quickly on the instrument.

WARNING! Is your child actually reading the music? Children are very clever at memorising bits very quickly which come easily. You'll be able to see if they take their eyes off the music and start looking at their hands. Naturally there may be the odd moment when they feel the need to look at their fingers, but this should be only momentary.

Memorise or Not?

What's wrong with memorising the music? Well, once the piece can be played without mistakes, then there's nothing wrong with memorising, but in practice, and while learning a piece from scratch, it can lead to wrong notes and rhythms slipping in. Your child may be totally unaware of the errors, and before you know it, the mistakes are memorised along with the rest of the piece...disaster!

Memorising just the easy bits can also lead to hesitations or gaps in the flow of the music as your child looks up at the music again and takes a moment to find their place on the page. These gaps can so easily get built into the piece, that they also go unnoticed, and become part of the piece!

If your child can play the correct notes and rhythm with no hesitations, then it will be memorised accurately.

Try to ensure accuracy with no gaps or hesitations before memorising a piece. Don't memorise mistakes!

Don't Always Practice from The Beginning

A child normally wants to start from the beginning of the piece every time, especially if this has become the norm. After all, that's usually the bit they can play well and feel most confident with.

However, they then begin to slow down and stumble as they hit the bit they don't know so well. Speed and continuity are lost.

Instead, try encouraging a start from various other suitable points, such as a repeat sign, or the start of a new phrase. Music is often written in four bar phrases and each one offers a reasonable starting place.

This helps children to learn a piece thoroughly and improves their skill in getting back into the piece if they make a mistake in a pressured situation, like a performance or an exam.

I have heard many children play through their piece perfectly, yet when I ask them to just play the second half or just the last line, they play as if they've never seen it before. Full of errors!

Quick Recap

- Make the most of the practice time you have. Have a pencil handy.
- Avoid stopping and starting your child too much during a play through. Let them play to the end before taking it apart to work on.
- Accurate repetition of a section or piece is the key to knowing it well.

- Use games to add fun and variety and consolidate learning.
- Aim for 15 or 20 minutes' practice 4 or 5 times each week, (if your child is young 10-15 mins).
- Teach the fingers where to go, slowly and accurately.
- Avoid memorising the easy bits. Read the music.
- Try starting from different places, not always from the beginning

CHAPTER SEVEN

Sight-Reading- how to stop it being a stumbling block.

Many children find this element very difficult. They feel under pressure and panic at the thought of having to play something, without having prepared fully.

What is it and how do you do it? Sight-reading involves playing a piece which has been put in front of you for the first time. In an examination situation, you would be given a short time (maximum of 30 seconds) to look the piece over before having to play it to the best of your ability. This skill requires fast reactions and a very cool head!

The temptation to go back and correct mistakes must be avoided. Any errors should be forgotten quickly so your child can focus on the rest of the piece. Accuracy of notes, rhythm, musical expression and phrasing are all taken into account when assessing a child's sight-reading skills.

The best way to improve sight-reading skills is to practice, practice, practice! This boosts confidence and greatly reduces the time it takes to learn new pieces. Start doing this at an early stage. Find some short easy pieces and get your child to have a go. Doing one or two each practice session, will really boost their sight-reading skills over time.

All face to face music exams will have a sight-reading test.

For the Initial Grade and Grades 1 and 2 it may only be four or eight bars long. For grades 3 and 4 it may be 12 or so bars.

During the short preparation time given, your child will be expected to recognise the rhythmic features. Find the starting note, observe any expression markings and of course get as many notes right as possible!

I have found that the biggest stumbling block is the child's mental attitude. It is very easy to panic and worry about getting the slightest thing wrong. This is especially true of the very conscientious child, who likes to get everything just right. This of course can lead to even more errors.

Below is my personal approach to getting the best out of sight-reading practice. It is by no means the only approach, but for a parent new to this concept, it may be a useful guide.

Try building in just one of the following elements at a time: rhythm, notes and expression markings. Focus on one, in each practice session.

A few minutes during the practice session should be spent on a line or so of music never seen before. Select something slightly easier than their current level of playing.

Rhythm

Start off by looking at how many beats there are in every bar, (notice the time signature). For example, 2 3 or 4 as the upper number in the time signature. Ask your child to tap or clap out the rhythm. Then play the rhythm on the instrument, using the same note all the way through. This saves having to think about too many things at once!

Your child can focus purely on the rhythm. If your child is familiar with using rhythmic sentences or words, then work out which ones fit the rhythmic figures in the sight-reading exercise, and use them appropriately.   Here are a couple of simple examples of words that your child can use.

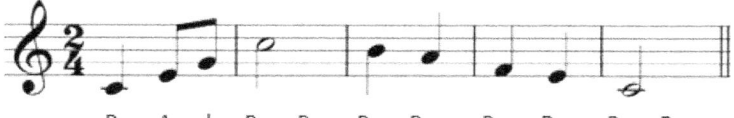

Pear App-le Pear Pear Pear Pear   Pear Pear   Pear Pear
Cat Dogg-ie Cat   Cat   Cat   Cat   Cat   Cat   Cat Cat

Know the Notes in no time!

Use the note finding sentences that are familiar. Remember, FACE for the Treble Clef, and All Cows Eat Grass for the Bass Clef. It doesn't matter about the different note values shown in the images below, what's important is the space or line the note sits on.

All   Cows   Eat   Grass

F A C E

Use these note reminders above to help find any notes your child may be uncertain of. Observe any patterns in the notes, for example, where they are the same, where they go up one, or down one etc. Sometimes you'll see numbers printed above or below notes. These are finger numbers, known as **fingerings** which will help your child put the right fingers on the notes. They are useful but don't have to be followed.

Give the fingers a 'dry run' of the more difficult looking bars if there's time. In exam conditions, your child is unlikely to have enough time to try the whole piece before being asked to play - unless it's the Initial Grade or Grade 1 - so encourage your child to use the preparation time wisely. Prioritise! Allow your child to simply focus solely on the notes. Don't worry at this stage about adding expression markings or rhythm.

Expression Markings - show off what you know!

These may be few or many depending on the piece given. For the purpose of practicing this as a sight-reading discipline, choose something that has several markings of expression such as **p** (play quietly), **f** (play loudly), **mp/mf** (play half quiet/half loud) etc. If your child doesn't know what something means, ask them to take a guess. Better to go with what they think than demonstrate nothing at all! Make a point though, of looking it up after the practice!

Get used to making the dynamics (louds and softs) and speed changes really noticeable. It's no good if it's barely audible. Remember, in an exam your child is there to show the examiner that they know what they are doing. Encourage your child to be bold and make sure they can be heard. I covered the basic expression instructions fully in chapter five.

Overcoming the Fear of Mistakes

Children don't like making mistakes and there's always a strong temptation to go back and correct it - usually with a bit of hesitation in between. This not only loses the rhythm and momentum of the piece but it also draws attention to your mistake. This can be a very difficult habit to overcome.

Far better to carry on maintaining the printed rhythm without drawing attention to the error. Even if your child knows he/she has played something wrong, encourage them to re-establish the rhythm and notes as quickly as possible.

There is a fun way to work on this skill. Simply take the sight-reading piece and play the correct printed rhythm, but with any old notes. Don't even attempt to play any correct notes. No need even to place the fingers in the correct starting position. Simply be interested in playing the correct rhythm.

Try to get your child complete the piece with the correct

rhythm and wrong notes and most importantly without hesitation or correction. This will feel totally alien at first but really can be a fun thing to do. It's like being allowed to break the rules!

I have used this method for many years and had great results. It helps to overcome the natural habit of going back over the error and correcting it. (After all we naturally want to show that we've realised our error and can actually do it correctly if given the chance).

This is all well and good when learning/practicing a piece of new music but when sight - reading skills are being tested and developed it's a different ball game. One must adapt to the requirements of the sight-reading discipline. Being able to play on, past a mistake you know you've made, without it putting you off, or playing on your mind and disrupting your concentration for the rest of the sight-reading material, is a skill which requires learning.

Try incorporating it as one of the practice disciplines to be used on a regular basis. It could work wonders for their ability to get through a piece of sight-reading during an exam without stopping or hesitating.

For more help, go to the ABRSM sight reading page for piano with lots of help and tips.

Quick recap

- Avoid hesitating after a mistake or going back to correct it.
- Practice sight-reading regularly.
- Separate rhythm, notes and expression in sight-reading practice.
- Focus on them one at a time. Until your child becomes more proficient.
- Scan the music quickly looking for patterns in notes and rhythm. Have a 'dry run' of the more difficult looking bits

CHAPTER EIGHT

Music Examinations. Will They Suite My Child?

Music examinations are of course, optional. You might have a child who thrives on exams, goals and targets. They might get a buzz from seeing their name on the certificate and moving up the Grades. Lucky you! These children will become more and more used to preparing the exam material to a high standard over a period of a few months. It requires determination and continuity in lessons and practice.

Or you might have a child for whom the mere thought of taking an exam is off- putting. Fear of failing and lack of confidence is often the cause. These children may still progress at a good rate, but need to find their sense of achievement in some other way. One option is to simply prepare the exam material without taking the exam itself. But if you're going to do this, you and the teacher need to choose pieces and studies carefully to maintain your child's interest. One of the advantages in taking an exam is that the material will need to be performed to a high standard. This requires careful and thorough preparation. Working on something to this level will give your child a sense of satisfaction and achievement.

Where? And When?

There are various examination boards and it will depend on the teacher as to which one they prefer. However, the most widely used is the Associated Board of the Royal Schools of Music, (ABRSM).

They hold their face to face exams three times a year, generally in February-March, June-July and November-December. You can take the exams at a child's school or an examination centre close by. This will largely depend on the teacher and how many pupils he/she is entering for any particular exam session.

In the past it was usually up to the teacher to enter children for exams, but the ABRSM upgraded their exam entry system recently and it now makes more sense for parents to enter their own child.

There is now also the option of entering your child for a Performance Grade. These Performance Grades are recorded by the parent or carer at home and the video is sent to the ABRSM for marking. These Performance exams have a date range for submission of the video. I will explain the differences in requirements between the face to face and Performance exams later on in this Chapter.

The exams are graded 1 - 8 and span one exam each year as a general rule. However, it is not uncommon for a child to skip a grade if they are moving at a particularly fast rate.

The Climb to Grade 1 May Be Steep.

You don't have to get your child to Grade 1 level all in one go. There are now two undercuts to Grade 1, the **Preparatory Test** (known as the Prep Test), and the **Initial Grade**. Both of which are achievable within the first year of learning (providing regular practice occurs at home between lessons). The Prep Test requires two short pieces to be played plus three very short finger exercises. There are also a couple of what they call listening tests (clapping and singing). **This is NOT a pass/fail test**. It was designed to give children a chance to experience a formal exam situation without the pressure of a marking system and a pass/fail result. I have found the Prep Test to be very popular with my pupils and highly recommend it. It gives your child an achievable goal to work towards after just a few months of learning.

The Initial Grade is quite new to the ABRSM's exam portfolio. It lines up much more closely with the Grade 1 requirements except at an easier level. So three pieces need to be prepared along with a few finger exercises (scales & arpeggios).

There is also the sight reading element, which requires your child to play a very short tune with just (up to) 30 seconds preparation time. Lastly there are listening tests, known as **aural tests** which again require some listening, clapping and singing. Unlike the Prep Test, this Initial Grade is a pass/fail exam. Each element is marked and your child will need a total of 100 to pass.

I have also found this Initial Grade to be very popular with pupils and parents and sets your child up very well for Grades 1-8 which follow. Certificates and mark sheets are issued for all exams.

Examination Preparation for Initial Grade & Grades 1-8

These may vary depending on which examination board you use, but for the ABRSM face to face exams, candidates are given a selection of set pieces from which three must be chosen and prepared for examination performance, plus the finger exercises, sight reading and aural tests.

Some teachers prefer to make the selection of pieces for their pupils, most involve the pupil in the final choice. Many pieces have a piano accompaniment (unless your instrument is piano, of course, in which case you perform alone.)

A selection of scales and various similar exercises have to be played from memory. It is unlikely that all the exercises will be asked for in the exam, but they should be prepared to a high standard. After all, you won't know which ones the examiner will choose to hear.

There's just one **sight-reading** test in which your child will need to perform a short piece he/she has never seen before. There's up to 30 seconds to prepare it, before playing it to the examiner. You can find plenty of helpful information from the ABRSM website. There are also four short **aural tests** which cover basic listening skills. These vary depending on the Grade being taken, but they generally involve clapping rhythms, singing a short melody played first by the examiner, and recognising changes made to a short phrase played by the examiner. Again, go to the ABRSM website for further information.

If your child has special needs, including Asperger's, Autism, Dyslexia, your child may be given extra time for the sight-reading test. Alternatively, he/she might get enlarged print for the sight-reading test. Speak to your teacher about this.

For **Performance Grades** which are recorded on video, your child will need to perform just four pieces and nothing else, no sight reading, scales/arpeggios, or aural tests. Instead the balance of the marks is allocated to the fourth piece and the standard of performance as a whole. Here's a link to the ABRSM website giving more information about Performance Grades and what's required: https://gb.abrsm.org/en/our-exams/performancegrades/

How is it marked?

Here's how the allocation of marks works out for **face to face exams.**

Piece 1	Min 20 max 30
Piece 2	Min 20 max 30
Piece 3	Min 20 max 30
Scales & Arpeggios	Min 14 max 21
Sight reading	Min 14 max 21
Aural tests	Min 12 max 18

Here's how the allocation of marks works out for **Performance Grades**

Piece 1	Min 20 max 30
Piece 2	Min 20 max 30
Piece 3	Min 20 max 30
Piece 4	Min 20 max 30
Performance as a whole	Min 20 max 30

Marks are graded 100-119 Pass, 120-129 Merit, 130-150 Distinction

CHAPTER NINE

Know the Lingo

This chapter explains a few of the more common classical terms, the kind of words you are likely to see in a concert programme for example, or at the top of a piece of music your child might be playing... Many of the terms give an indication of speed and character of the music, others express the type of occasion the music was most suited to.

As you will already know from Chapter five 'Express Yourself', many musical terms are Italian. Here are some brief explanations which will give you a start and may even help you answer the odd crossword clue!

Adagio	This is often used to title a piece, meaning slow, at ease. A piece which is divided into movements, such as in a symphony, often has an Adagio.
Allegro	This is often used as the title of a piece. It means quick and lively. Often used as a title of a piece or movement.
Andante	Often used as the title of a piece. It means, moving along, at a walking pace. Often used to title a piece or movement.
Concerto	A piece usually in three movements for a solo instrument with an orchestral accompaniment (which is often adapted for piano).
Divertimento	Sometimes used as the title of a piece. A suite of short

	movements written for a small group of players. Usually light and less serious in style.
Gavotte	Often used as the title of a piece. Originally a French dance with four beats in every bar, beginning on the third beat of the bar.
Gigue	Often used as the title of a short piece. A French jig, lively and rustic in style
Harmony	Chords which either stand alone or accompany a melody
Intermezzo	Originally this was a short piece of light musical entertainment performed between acts of a play or more serious music. Later it began to appear as a short movement in a symphony, or concerto.
Largo	Often used as a title of a piece of music, it denotes the character of the piece as slow and broad.
Minuet	Often used as the title of a piece. It is a dance with three beats in every bar, a very early prelude to the waltz
Prelude	This is sometimes used to title a piece. It's a short piece that introduces the main feature.
Serenade	Sometimes used to title a piece. Originally it was played in honour of someone. Usually performed by small groups such as a string or wind ensemble
Sonata	Originally known as music for

	instruments, as opposed to voice. It has several movements and usually as soloist.
Sonatina	A short Sonata
Symphony	A piece for a large orchestra, usually with four movements.

CONCLUSION

This guide should hopefully take the pain out of practicing for both you and your child. It's not easy for you as a parent, if you don't play an instrument yourself, to help your children practice.

Hopefully you'll be able to do that now. And it might even give you the music bug yourself!

I also hope that this book has given a clear indication of the time and commitment required from both child and parent to progress with an instrument. Your child may have come home from on school asking to take up an instrument on a whim, but in truth your child will only progress and get pleasure from learning, if enough time is given to nurturing your child's musical progress at home. It doesn't matter if you (the parent), know nothing about music, that's precisely why I wrote this little book - to give you enough tools to help at home with confidence.

I've seen too many children give up their instrument over the years due to being left to their own devices and getting little or no help/support at home from a mum or dad. Sometimes, all it takes is to sit with your child for 10/15 mins while they play you their latest or favourite tunes. Recording a little video of your child playing, and sending it to other family members or friends can make all the difference to a young budding musician who needs a little recognition for their musical efforts.

My sincerest thanks for reading this Guide and I hope it has given you some helpful tips and hints and above all encouragement for you the parent

TESTIMONIALS, WHAT PARENTS SAY

Ruth's approach is excellent! My 7 year old son is really enjoying learning to play the violin and I have no doubt that his enjoyment and the great progress he is making is due to the practice methods that Ruth has encouraged him to adopt. As a parent, I was expecting encouraging practice to be a challenge, but Ruth has really helped to make this easier...and fun for both of us!

Jenny Peters

Ruth's advice to keep practice sessions short but regular has been particularly effective and the tips for making practice fun have helped my son stay motivated, even when learning a particularly tricky piece. Learning scales has also been much easier than I expected. Ruth notates scales in an easy to read format which I am sure explains why he has learnt them more quickly and easily than I ever did!

Sarah Fearn

My daughter has been having violin lessons with Ruth now for nearly a year and a half, having previously had disjointed and lacklustre lessons at school. Ruth has transformed Darcey's technique and performance skills and given Darcey confidence and enthusiasm to push herself to show her growing skills off regularly at school in concerts, assemblies & even talent shows. Ruth's attention to detail extends beyond her lessons always providing invaluable tips and support for practice at home, everything from simply practicing in front of the mirror (to improve arm and bowing positions); to constructing a scale wheel as a fun way of tackling scales in bit size portions. I never hesitate in recommending Ruth and her frequent theory workshops are also an invaluable additional support to her instrumental lessons.

Elaine Florsheim

'The key areas that Ruth has set out concerning practice have been really useful in ensuring that Seb makes best use of practice time on his violin during the week, in between lessons. It is so easy for children to get into bad habits. If we do not oversee practice and enthuse with sound advice from Ruth then our children will not progress a fast as they might. Well worth listening to what Ruth says in her helpful tips.'

Mike Wallis

Ruth has been a great inspiration for my daughter. She has taught her to play the violin beautifully and expertly guided her through the examinations. She has provided extra lessons when required and has been very flexible with times and dates. My daughter really enjoys her lessons and I've been very impressed with the rapid progress she has made. She has a very lovely teaching style. I really can't recommend her highly enough!

Julie Robinson

Useful Notes & Reminders for Music Practice

Useful Notes & Reminders for Music Practice

Useful Notes & Reminders for Music Practice

Printed in Great Britain
by Amazon

34439885R00050